What Is a ▮

Lola M. Scha▮▮▮

giant panda

Consulting Editor: Gail Saunders-Smith, Ph.D.

Consultant: Dwight Lawson, Ph.D.
General Curator, Zoo Atlanta

Pebble Books

an imprint of Capstone Press
Mankato, Minnesota

Pebble Books are published by Capstone Press
151 Good Counsel Drive, P.O. Box 669, Mankato, Minnesota 56002
http://www.capstone-press.com

1 2 3 4 5 6 06 05 04 03 02 01

Library of Congress Cataloging-in-Publication Data
Schaefer, Lola M., 1950–
    What is a mammal?/by Lola M. Schaefer.
    p. cm.—(The Animal Kingdom)
    Includes bibliographical references (p. 23) and index.
    ISBN 0-7368-0867-1
    1. Mammals—Juvenile literature. [1. Mammals.] I. Title. II. Series.
QL706.2 .S33 2001
599—dc21   00-009672

Summary: Simple text and photographs present mammals and their general
characteristics.

Note to Parents and Teachers

The Animal Kingdom series supports national science standards
related to the diversity of living things. This book describes and
illustrates mammals and their general characteristics. The
photographs support early readers in understanding the text. The
repetition of words and phrases helps early readers learn new
words. This book also introduces early readers to subject-specific
vocabulary words, which are defined in the Words to Know section.
Early readers may need assistance to read some words and to use
the Table of Contents, Words to Know, Read More, Internet Sites,
and Index/Word List sections of the book.

Table of Contents

elephant

4

dolphins

Mammals are part of the animal kingdom. Most mammals live on land. Some mammals live in water.

giraffe

polar bear

Mammals are warm-blooded. Their body temperature stays the same in all surroundings.

Mammals have a skeleton.

kangaroo

lungs

Mammals breathe air through lungs.

human

walrus

wolf

tiger

bear

12

Mammals have hair.

monkey

zebras

bat

14

sea lion

Most mammals have four limbs. Mammals can have arms, legs, wings, or flippers.

dog

cat

Many mammals have tails.

Most female mammals give birth to young.

gorilla with young

Female mammals nurse their young.

pig with piglets

Words to Know

animal kingdom—the group that includes all animals

female—an animal that can give birth to young animals or lay eggs

limb—a body part used to move or grasp; arms, legs, wings, and flippers are kinds of animal limbs.

lung—a body part in the chest that animals use to breathe

nurse—to feed a young animal milk from its mother

skeleton—a framework of bones in a body

temperature—the measure of how hot or cold something is

warm-blooded—having a body temperature that stays about the same, no matter what the outside temperature is; birds and mammals are warm-blooded animals.

Read More

Franchino, Vicki. *Mammals.* Simply Science. Minneapolis: Compass Point Books, 2000.

Kalman, Bobbie. *What Is a Mammal?* The Science of Living Things. New York: Crabtree Publishing, 1998.

Savage, Stephen. *Mammals.* What's the Difference? Austin, Texas: Raintree Steck-Vaughn, 2000.

Internet Sites

All about Mammals
http://www.EnchantedLearning.com/
subjects/mammals

Animal Bytes
http://www.seaworld.org/animal_bytes/
animal_bytes.html

Animals of the World
http://www.kidscom.com/orakc/Games/
Animalgame/index.html

Classifying Critters
http://www.hhmi.org/coolscience/critters/critters.html

Index/Word List

Word Count: 70
Early-Intervention Level: 9

Editorial Credits

Mari C. Schuh, editor; Kia Bielke, cover designer and illustrator; Marilyn Moseley LaMantia, illustrator (page 10); Kimberly Danger, photo researcher

Photo Credits

Brandon D. Cole, 4 (bottom)
Corel Corporation, cover (upper right, lower right, and upper left), 1, 4 (top), 6 (both), 12 (upper right, lower left, and lower right), 16 (both)
FPG International LLC, cover (lower left)
Fritz Polking/Bruce Coleman Inc., 18
Index Stock Imagery, 20
Joe McDonald/McDonald Wildlife Photography, 12 (upper left)
Joe McDonald/Tom Stack & Associates, 14 (lower left)
Leonard Rue Enterprises, 8
Marilyn Moseley LaMantia, 10
PhotoDisc, Inc., 14 (upper left, upper right, and lower right)